Wouldn't
Have Been More Sensible?

Wouldn't a Gremlin Have Been More Sensible?

a *Doonesbury* book by G. B. Trudeau

Holt, Rinehart and Winston
New York

Published simultaneously in Canada by Holt, Rinehart
and Winston of Canada, Limited.
Library of Congress Catalog Card Number: 75-922
ISBN: 0-03-014901-0
First Edition
Printed in the United States of America
The cartoons in this book have appeared in newspapers
in the United States and abroad under the auspices of
Universal Press Syndicate.

OUR REGULARLY SCHEDULED PROGRAM WILL NOT BE SEEN TONIGHT IN ORDER TO BRING YOU AN *NBC NEWS SPECIAL REPORT!*

GOOD EVENING. I'M JOHN CHANCELLOR. THE BUILDING YOU SEE BEHIND ME IS THE UNITED STATES TREASURY.

DEEP IN THE BOWELS OF THAT AUSTERE EDIFICE, THERE IS A MAN WHO EVEN NOW WORKS FEVERISHLY TO SALVAGE OUR FALTERING ECONOMY. THAT MAN IS THE SUBJECT OF TONIGHT'S *NBC CLOSE-UP!*

CZAR! THE MAN AND THE MONEY!

BROUGHT TO YOU BY...

SITWELL, PENNSYLVANIA. POPULATION 1,733. THIS IS WHERE THE BOY CZAR SPENT HIS YOUTH — MAKING TREE FORTS, PLAYING KICK THE CAN, BUILDING UP HIS FIRST PORTFOLIO.

THE CZAR'S FATHER, ALBERT. I'LL NEVER FORGET THE DAY HE BOUGHT HIS FIRST TEN SHARES OF COMMON STOCK. IT WAS IN A STRUGGLING NEW COMPANY CALLED IBM.

I HAVE TO ADMIT THAT AT THE TIME I DISAPPROVED. I TOLD HIM THE INVESTMENT WAS CHANCEY, DICEY — THAT I WOULDN'T PUT A PENNY INTO A COMPANY LIKE THAT!

THAT PROBABLY EXPLAINS WHY I'M STILL LIVING IN A MOBILE HOME.

WALL STREET. NEW YORK'S YELLOW BRICK ROAD. THE PLACE WHERE A THOUSAND DREAMS ARE REALIZED OR SHATTERED. IT WAS HERE THE YOUNG CZAR FIRST CAME TO SEEK HIS FORTUNE.

BROKERS, INDUSTRIALISTS, BANKERS, MONEY MAGNATES OF ALL KINDS — THESE ARE BILL SIMON'S PEOPLE. THESE ARE THE PEOPLE WHO WATCHED AS HE COOLLY WENT ABOUT MAKING HIS FIRST MILLION.

ALBIE ROBERTS, A FELLOW BROKER IN THE CZAR'S OLD FIRM. THE GUY WAS A BUM. HE'D SELL HIS OWN CHILDREN IF THE MARKET WERE RIGHT.

YES, IT'S A TOUGH SCENE, WALL STREET..

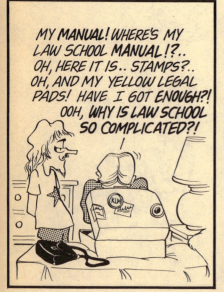

SON, THEY SAY WHEN A MAN THINKS HE'S ABOUT TO DIE HIS WHOLE LIFE PASSES BEFORE HIS EYES..

BUT YOU KNOW WHAT HAPPENED TO ME? WHEN I FELT THAT SHARP PAIN IN MY CHEST, SUDDENLY MY WHOLE STOCK PORTFOLIO PASSED BEFORE MY EYES — AND THE PRICES WERE PLUMMETING!

IN THE BACK OF MY MIND A LITTLE VOICE STARTED YELLING, "SELL! SELL!," AND UP ON A BIG BOARD THE DOW JONES BEGAN TO DIVE — 800! 700! 600! 500! 400! 300!

I BLACKED OUT AT 180.

I'LL BET.

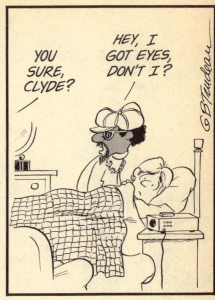

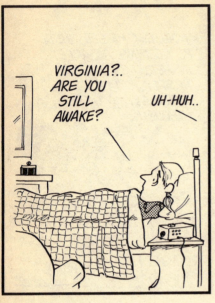

"ANYWAY, IN SPITE OF HER BOYFRIEND, VIRGINIA IS A VERY SPECIAL PERSON, AND I FEEL LUCKY TO HAVE HER AS MY ROOMMATE."

"THE FIRST DAYS OF CLASSES HAVE BEEN INTERESTING. I HAVE TWO MALE PROFESSORS, ONE FEMALE PROFESSOR, AND ONE GAY DISCUSSION-GROUP LEADER..."

"THEY ALL SEEM LIKE PRETTY GOOD PEOPLE, EXCEPT FOR ONE OF THE MALE TEACHERS, PROFESSOR LATHRAP. IN DE-SCRIBING HIM, THE WORD THAT COMES MOST READILY TO MIND IS 'PIG'."

NOW REMEMBER— THE PINK ASSIGNMENT SHEETS ARE FOR THE GIRLS; BLUE FOR THE BOYS!

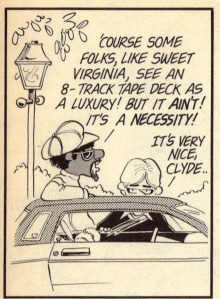

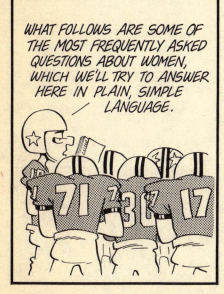

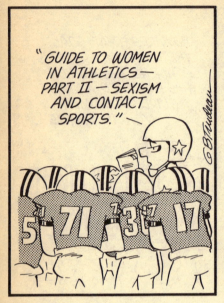

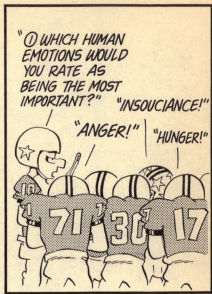

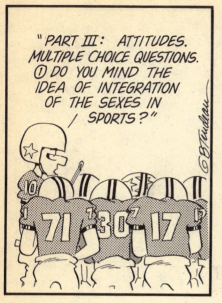

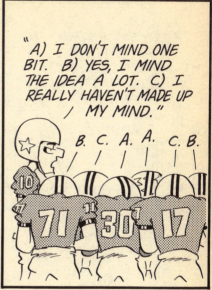

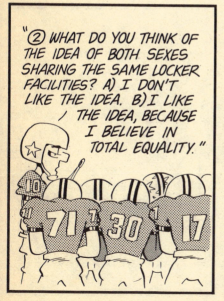

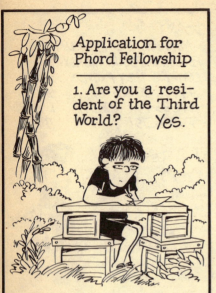

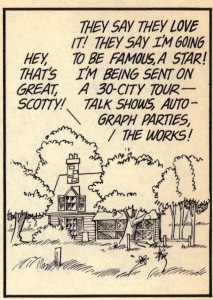

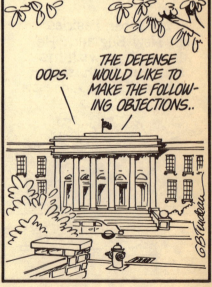

Dear Mr. President,

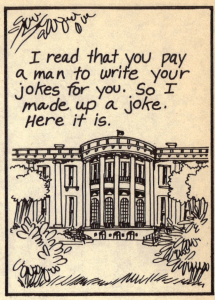

I read that you pay a man to write your jokes for you. So I made up a joke. Here it is.

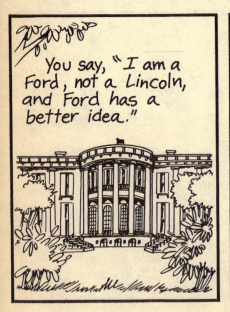

You say, "I am a Ford, not a Lincoln, and Ford has a better idea."

Please pay me $10.00 for this joke. Your friend, Billy R.

Dear Mr. President,
I heard that if I wrote
you I would get a
personal letter back.

I will be honest with you.
Right now I have no
friends at school. But if
I had a letter from you
everyone would want to
be my friend.

Please use paper that says
the White House so that the
kids won't think I wrote it
myself to trick them. Also,
please write a personal
P.S., sort of kidding around
and stuff.

This better
work.

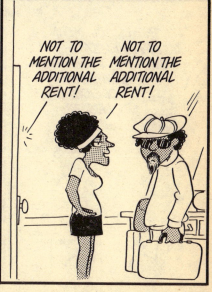

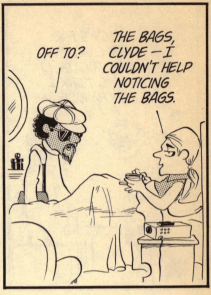

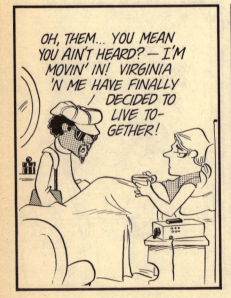

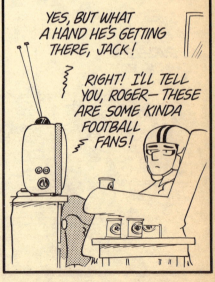

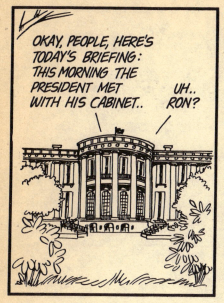

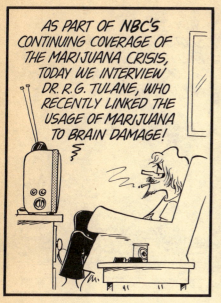